41X(3-19)/520

✓MM

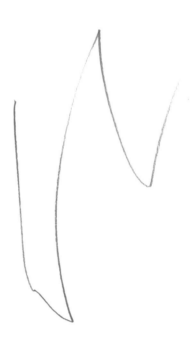

PEOPLES OF THE ANCIENT WORLD

Life in Ancient Egypt

Paul Challen

Crabtree Publishing Company
www.crabtreebooks.com

Crabtree Publishing Company
www.crabtreebooks.com

For Sam, Evelina, and Henry

Coordinating editor: Ellen Rodger
Project editor: Sean Charlebois
Editors: Rachel Eagen, Carrie Gleason, Adrianna Morganelli
Production coordinator: Rosie Gowsell
Production assistance: Samara Parent
Scanning technician: Arlene Arch-Wilson
Photo research: Allison Napier
Art director: Rob MacGregor

Project management assistance:
Media Projects, Inc.
Carter Smith
Pat Smith
Laura Smyth
Aimee Kraus
Michael Greenhut

Consultant: Roberta L. Shaw, Assistant Curator, Egyptology Section, Royal Ontario Museum

Barbara Richman, Farragut Middle School, Hastings-on-Hudson NY

Photographs: Archivo Iconografico, S.A./CORBIS: p. 8; Bettmann/CORBIS: p. 25, p. 30; Art Resource, NY: p. 17; Borromeo / Art Resource, NY: p. 13; Peter Crabtree: p. 5, p. 7, pp. 10–11, p. 16, p. 18 (right), p. 19 (both), p. 24; Fotosearch/Corel: pp. 4-5 (left); Giraudon / Art Resource, NY: p. 17; Charles & Josette Lenars/CORBIS: p. 12; Erich Lessing/Art Resource, NY: p. 15 (both); Winnifred Neeler, Royal Ontario Museum: p. 13 (bottom); North Carolina Museum of Art/CORBIS: p. 30; Richard T. Nowitz/CORBIS: p. 23; Gianni Dagli Orti/CORBIS: p. 3, p. 22, p. 23; Roger Wood/CORBIS: p. 7, p. 9; Sandro Vannini/CORBIS; Werner Forman / Art Resource, NY: p. 22, p. 23

Illustrations: Roman Goforth: p. 1, p. 5 (icon), p. 8, p. 13 (top), p. 14 (all), p. 15 (bottom), pp. 20-21, pp. 26-27 (inset); Rosie Gowsell: borders, p. 16 (top); Rob MacGregor: pp. 4–5 (timeline), p. 6 (map), p. 11, p. 29 (top)

Cartography: Jim Chernishenko: p. 6

Cover: A throne found in the tomb of Pharaoh Tutenkhamen.

Contents: Wealthy Egyptians and their families hunted on the Nile River.

Title page: The ancient Egyptians mummified, or preserved their dead.

Crabtree Publishing Company
www.crabtreebooks.com   1-800-387-7650

Cataloging-in-Publication Data

Challen, Paul C. (Paul Clarence), 1967-
  Life in ancient Egypt / written by Paul Challen.
     p. cm. -- (Peoples of the ancient world)
  Includes index.
  ISBN 0-7787-2038-1 (rlb.) -- ISBN 0-7787-2068-3 (pbk.)
  1. Egypt--Civilization--To 332 B.C.--Juvenile literature. 2. Egypt--Civilization--332 B.C.-638 A.D.--Juvenile literature.
I. Title. II. Series.
  DT61.C42 2004
  932--dc22

                                        2004013068
                                              LC

**Published in
the United States**
PMB 16A
350 Fifth Ave.
Suite 3308
New York, NY
10118

**Published
in Canada**
612 Welland Ave.,
St. Catharines,
Ontario, Canada
L2M 5V6

**Published in the
United Kingdom**
73 Lime Walk
Headington
Oxford
0X3 7AD
United Kingdom

**Published
in Australia**
386 Mt. Alexander Rd.,
Ascot Vale (Melbourne)
V1C 3032

Contents

On the River Nile

No one knows for certain when the first people settled in Egypt, but its civilization is one of the oldest in human history. The first settlements grew on the banks of the Nile River about 7,000 years ago. Over time, and until its defeat by the Roman Empire **in 30 B.C., Egypt became one of the greatest of the ancient** cultures.

Ancient Egypt was ruled by a series of kings, or pharaohs, who were thought to be the representatives of the gods on earth. The power to rule was kept in the family, or dynasty. A pharaoh usually passed his position on to his son, who passed it on to the next **generation**. From about 2650 B.C. to 1500 B.C., dead pharaohs were buried in enormous stone structures called **pyramids** that took many years and thousands of workers to build. Workers also built great cities throughout Egypt, including Karnak, Thebes, Luxor, and Memphis.

High Achievers

Ancient Egyptians are famous for a process of preserving the dead called mummification. Writers called scribes wrote laws and history using a system of writing known as hieroglyphs. Ancient Egyptian farmers made tools to use the waters of the Nile River to **irrigate** their fields.

▶ *The Great Pyramids at Giza were built 4,500 years ago from massive blocks of limestone.*

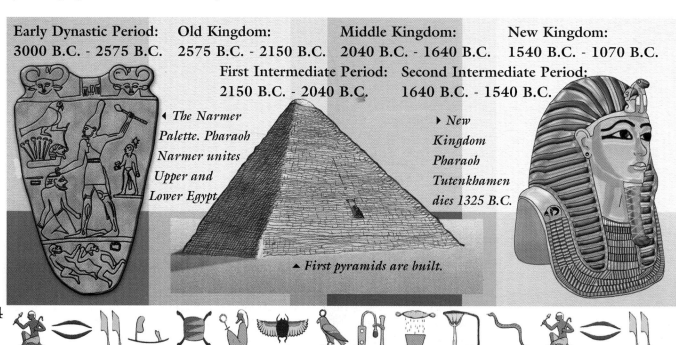

Early Dynastic Period:	Old Kingdom:	Middle Kingdom:	New Kingdom:
3000 B.C. - 2575 B.C.	2575 B.C. - 2150 B.C.	2040 B.C. - 1640 B.C.	1540 B.C. - 1070 B.C.
	First Intermediate Period:	Second Intermediate Period:	
	2150 B.C. - 2040 B.C.	1640 B.C. - 1540 B.C.	

◀ *The Narmer Palette. Pharaoh Narmer unites Upper and Lower Egypt.*

▶ *New Kingdom Pharaoh Tutenkhamen dies 1325 B.C.*

▲ *First pyramids are built.*

Invading Enemies

To Egypt's north lay the Mediterranean Sea, which armies from foreign lands sometimes crossed with ships to invade Egypt. To the south and east lay other enemies who also invaded Egypt. Despite being surrounded by neighbors who fought over the land, Egyptian civilization endured for thousands of years.

▲ *Many historians believe that the face of the Sphinx is the face of the Pharaoh Chephren. The Sphinx, a half man, half lion figure guards the causeway, or tunnel, to the pharaoh's tomb.*

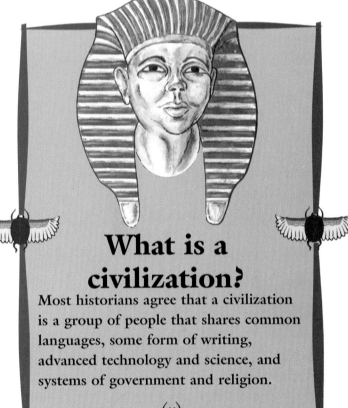

What is a civilization?

Most historians agree that a civilization is a group of people that shares common languages, some form of writing, advanced technology and science, and systems of government and religion.

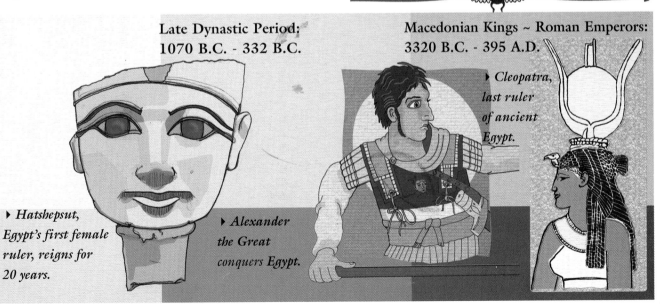

Late Dynastic Period:
1070 B.C. - 332 B.C.

Macedonian Kings ~ Roman Emperors:
3320 B.C. - 395 A.D.

▶ *Cleopatra, last ruler of ancient Egypt.*

▶ *Hatshepsut, Egypt's first female ruler, reigns for 20 years.*

▶ *Alexander the Great conquers Egypt.*

The Black Land

Egyptian civilization would not have developed without the Nile River. The ancient Egyptians' name for their land was Kemet, the "black land," because of the rich black mud left on the river banks after the mid-summer floods receded. The soil in the Nile River Valley was very fertile for farming.

The River Delta

The Nile is the longest river in the world. The Nile flows northward from central Africa for 4,150 miles (6,679 km) before emptying into the Mediterranean Sea. The triangle where the river meets the sea is known as the Nile delta. The area around the delta was known as Lower Egypt. The area to the south was called Upper Egypt.

Every year from July to October, rain caused the Nile to flood and leave muddy soil behind. In this rich soil farmers grew fruits and vegetables. The river supplied water for **pastures** where farmers raised animals. A plant called papyrus grew in the river's marshes and was used to make paper. Papyrus stalks were used to build river boats for fishing. The boats sailed the Nile, allowing Egyptians to trade with neighboring peoples.

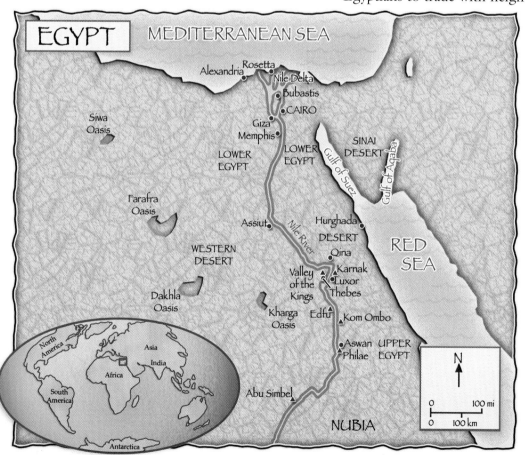

◀ *Most of Egypt's land is desert. The area around the Nile, known as the delta, was excellent for growing crops.*

The Red Land

Only the very narrow strip on each side of the Nile River was suitable for farming. Land beyond the river banks was scorching desert, known as the red lands. The red lands were a source of copper, gold and other **minerals** used to make jewelry and tools.

The Pharaoh and the River

Egyptians believed their pharaoh controlled the weather and the Nile. They thought he was the only one who could please Hapi, the flood god, and guarantee a supply of water for growing crops. Without the flood, there would be famine.

▼ *The ancient Egyptians farmed the banks of the Nile just as they are farmed today.*

The Egyptian seasons

There were three seasons each year in ancient Egypt. The flood season, from July to October, was called Akhet. Farmers could not grow food during Akhet because fields were flooded. Instead, they fixed tools and prepared for Peret, the season when the waters receded and crops could be planted. During Shemu, from March to June, farmers worked very long hours harvesting crops.

▲ *The Nile was home to many kinds of wildlife. When the waters rose too high to farm, Egyptians, like this wealthy family, hunted wild birds.*

Egyptian Empire

Historians divide Egypt's history into three periods: Old Kingdom (2700 B.C. to 2200 B.C.), Middle Kingdom (2000 B.C. to 1800 B.C.), and New Kingdom (1600 B.C. to 1100 B.C.). Each kingdom was ruled by dynasties, or family groups, for hundreds of years.

Before the Old Kingdom

The period of time before the Old Kingdom is called the Pre-Dynastic Period (3100 B.C. to 2686 B.C.). During this time, **nomadic hunters** began to settle permanently on the banks of the Nile. They grew crops and developed an early form of writing. These early Egyptians buried their kings under large flat slabs of dried mud called mastabas, or benches.

Two Kingdoms

Early Egypt was divided into two kingdoms, Upper Egypt and Lower Egypt. Pharaohs in Upper Egypt wore white crowns and those in Lower Egypt wore red crowns. Around 3100 B.C., a pharaoh named Narmer from Upper Egypt united the two kingdoms. Historians believe that Narmer was also known as Menes, since pharaohs often had several names. Narmer and those who followed his rule in the first and second dynasties had power for about 400 years.

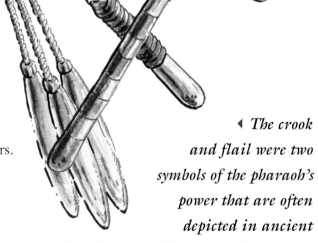

The Narmer Palette is a slab of stone that marks the victory of the Pharaoh Narmer. Narmer united the two kingdoms of Upper and Lower Egypt after a great battle.

◀ *The crook and flail were two symbols of the pharaoh's power that are often depicted in ancient Egyptian art. Pharaohs had the power to order punishments such as beatings.*

The Old Kingdom

Pharaohs became very powerful during the Old Kingdom. Pharaohs were often brave warriors who commanded the army. Strong military leadership was important to Egyptians since their kingdoms were sometimes attacked by their neighbors. Pharaohs also directed trade with other nations, made laws, and punished those who broke them. Punishments included fines, hard labor, beatings, and even death. Royal advisors called viziers and low-level officials from all over Egypt helped the pharaoh with his daily work of governing.

▼ *A model of the Nubian army found in a tomb shows the fierce warriors Egyptians battled with and conquered in the Middle Kingdom. During war, all Egyptian men served in the military and pharaohs hired foreign soldiers called mercenaries, to fight with them.*

The Middle Kingdom

The pharaoh decided which family member would succeed him after his death. Pharaoh Pepi II ruled for over 90 years but did not name an heir before he died. Many kings fought to claim control of Egypt after his death. This time of war is called the First Intermediate Period. By 2040 B.C., princes from the city of Thebes in Upper Egypt had gained control. This era is known as the Middle Kingdom. Egypt built a strong army to conquer the neighboring lands of Nubia and Kush in the south. At first, Egyptians used only shields, swords, and spears. By the 13th dynasty, when a people called the Hyksos defeated Egypt, Egyptians had learned how to use horses and chariots to help them in battle. Pharaohs hired foreign soldiers, called mercenaries, to help in battle. The Hyksos victory marked the end of the Middle Kingdom.

The New Kingdom

The New Kingdom is best known for three pharaohs: Hatshepsut, Akhenaton, and Ramses II. During the New Kingdom, Egypt reached the height of its power.

Amenhotep IV was a pharaoh who believed that the New Kingdom pharaohs who came before him had surrendered too much of their religious power to the **priests** who ran temples. To change this, Amenhotep IV ordered Egyptians to follow only one god. He chose his favorite, Aten, instead of Amun-Re, the chief god of all Egypt.

Amenhotep also changed his name to Akhenaton which meant "agreeable to Aten." He removed all traces of Amun-Re and put the symbol of Aten on monuments. Akhenaton declared that since he was Aten's representative, everyone should worship him. Akhenaton died an unpopular pharaoh and his successor, Tutenkhamen, restored Amun-Re.

The Decline

Pharaoh Ramses II was another New Kingdom ruler who considered himself a great warrior. Ramses II tried to win back lands lost during wars in Akhenaton's reign.

After Ramses II, assaults on Egypt became far more common. Ramses III defended Egypt against attackers from the Mediterranean called the "Sea People." Although Egypt won the battles, it was seriously weakened. It could no longer conquer other lands. From this time on, Egypt failed to fend off attacks by invaders and eventually came to be ruled by others.

▼ *Ramses II placed four giant statues of himself in front of one of his temples at Abu Simbel. Each one is an astounding 65 feet (20 meters) tall.*

Hatshepsut

Hatshepsut was the main wife of Thutmose II. After he died without an heir, she wore the clothing of kings and a false beard to become pharaoh. Hatshepsut was very successful and ruled for twenty years. She strengthened the navy and sent trade missions to the African coast.

11

Egyptian Economy

In the fertile Nile soil, farmers grew food for the Egyptians, including merchants who sailed the Nile's waters and builders who constructed canals and cities on its banks. The pharaoh taxed everyone, from traders to craftsmen and farmers. Taxes paid for the army, the government, and temples.

Agriculture

Egyptian farmers grew wheat, barley, peas, beans, onions, garlic, leeks, cucumbers, grapes, melons, pomegranates, figs, and dates to feed the growing population. They used the Nile's water to irrigate dry land. A network of irrigation canals supplied crops grown farthest away from the river with water.

When farmers sowed seeds, they drove herds of sheep or other animals over the ground to push the seeds down. During harvest time, all available workers, including soldiers, harvested the grain. With good irrigation, Egyptian farmers grew more grain than was needed to feed themselves, the army, and the workers who built the pharaoh's temples. The surplus seeds and grain were **bartered** for other goods with peoples to the south where wheat could not be easily grown.

▲ A 3,000-year-old papyrus painting shows farmers harvesting grain by hand.

▼ Egyptians used a tool called a shaduf to lift water from the Nile to the irrigation canals near fields.

Taxation

Pharaohs were very rich and added to their wealth every year in order to maintain their empire. To avoid using their own fortune, pharaohs taxed Egyptians to pay the government officials, soldiers, and craftsmen who worked for them. The pharaoh also decreed that conquered people from all over his empire pay him a tribute, or tax.

The pharaoh owned all the farmland in his kingdom. He ordered farmers to give him a portion of the crops they grew. Hunters and fishermen paid a tax with a portion of what they caught. There were no coins or money, so citizens could also pay their taxes by working on building projects such as canals, temples, pyramids, or statues that honored their leader or their gods.

Trade

Ships made of reed, papyrus, and wood sailed the Nile, carrying goods for trade. Egyptians traded objects crafted from gold, as well papyrus for writing, with people who lived up the Nile and across the sea.

Merchants used a system called barter in which people traded one item they possessed for another they needed. They traded for wine and oil from the island of Crete, in the Mediterranean Sea. Timber, tin, and horses were purchased from the eastern part of the Egyptian Empire. Copper for making tools came from Sinai, a peninsula on the northern end of the Red Sea to Egypt's east. Salt, dates, reeds, and cattle came from the desert oases. Gold, copper, amethyst, and cattle came from Nubia, a desert to the south and an incense called myrrh came from Punt, a desert in East Africa.

▼ Meketre, a wealthy noble, oversees workers as they drive his cattle to graze in the lush Delta area. This colorful 4,000-year-old model was placed in Meketre's tomb. Only the wealthiest Egyptians could afford such large herds of cattle.

▲ Egyptian slaves and servants worked in the homes and kitchens of nobles.

Everyday Life

Egyptian pharaohs were wealthy and powerful. Egyptians believed the pharaoh and his family should be treated like gods.

Who's On Top?

Even a pharaoh's closest advisor, called a vizier, treated him like a god. The pharaoh and his family were the most powerful members of Egyptian society. The pharaoh's vizier made sure the pharaoh's orders were carried out. A group of **nobles** and a small group of priests, soldiers, and government officials worked under the vizier. Everyday life in Egypt depended on the millions of laborers at the bottom of society, including slaves, servants, and farmers who worked in homes and fields. Farmers made sure crops were grown and harvested in Egypt; servants and slaves looked after the pharaoh and nobles by cooking, by cleaning, and by dressing them.

Women in Egypt

Women in ancient Egypt were expected to teach daughters in the home but many also had other jobs. Some women served in the pharaoh's palace as acrobats, dancers, singers, and musicians. Others worked for wealthy families as maids. Women could not hold government positions or inherit the title of pharaoh. Queen Hatshepsut ignored this rule and governed Egypt after the death of her husband Pharaoh Thutmose II. She had to dress like a man in order to keep power.

Slavery

Ancient Egyptians kept slaves who were considered the property of their masters. Most slaves were non-Egyptians captured in war. Slaves were forced to labor in the copper and gold mines of Sinai and Nubia. Other slaves were forced to fight in the Egyptian army or work for nobles.

Egyptian Social Pyramid

Pharaoh

Viziers

Priests

Scribes

Soldiers

Artisans

Farmers

Slaves and Servants

Home Sweet Home

Egyptian pharaohs and nobles lived in large homes made of stone, tile, and sun-baked bricks. The huts of farmers and craftsmen were made from mud and straw bricks that were dried in the sun and later painted white. Homes of farmers were only one or two rooms, while pharaohs and nobles had living quarters with shrines, banquet rooms, painted audience halls, broad corridors, balconies, formal gardens and pools, workshops, breweries, and stables.

▼ *The son and daughter of a royal priest and scribe named Nakt are shown in these details from a painting on the wall of Nakt's tomb in Thebes.*

A Child's Life

Only boys from wealthy or noble families attended school. They learned how to write with ink on papyrus and by carving hieroglyphs into pieces of clay. Older boys studied history, geography, science, and mathematics. Other boys learned a trade or craft from their fathers. Girls stayed home with their mothers and learned cooking and other skills they would need to run a household. Girls did not attend school, but girls from wealthy families were taught to read and write, and helped manage the estate. Some even trained at home to become doctors. Children also cared for elderly parents. Upon their parents' death, both sons and daughters **inherited** land.

Clothing

Egypt's hot weather required comfortable clothing. Ancient Egyptians wore clothing made from linen, a strong fabric made from the fibers of flax plants. Women wore long dresses while men often wore a kilt wrapped at the waist. When it was cooler, people wore a thick cloak over these light garments. Nobles wore leather sandals. Farmers and servants either did not wear shoes or wore sandals made from the tough stalks of Nile reed plants. Nobles at court and wealthy citizens wore wigs and fancy headdresses with beads and jewelry of gold and gemstones. Officials wore many elaborate necklaces, forming a broad collar.

Ancient Egyptians were among the first to develop a written language. They borrowed a system from people who lived in Mesopotamia, in modern-day Iraq, and adapted it for their own use.

▶ *Egyptian hieroglyphs used pictures to represent letters of the alphabet.*

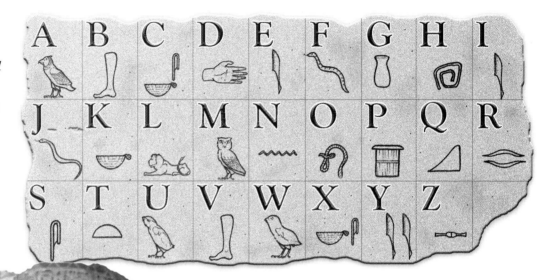

Hieroglyphs

The Egyptians believed their written language was a gift from Thoth, god of wisdom. They thought writing was a holy process. The writing was later called hieroglyphs, or "sacred carvings," because they were often carved in stone on temple walls. A shortened version of hieroglyphs, called hieratic script, was used by priests.

The Egyptians used a writing system of more than 700 symbols, each representing an entire word, a syllable, or a letter of the alphabet. There were no vowels or punctuation. Often, hieroglyph "words" combined two symbols with sounds that people already knew to make one word. For example, to express the name of King Narmer, Egyptians drew a symbol of a fish, "nar" over a chisel, "mer."

◀ *An obelisk with an image of an ancient Egyptian noble and hieroglyphs that tell a story.*

The Scribe

Very few people could read in ancient Egypt. Young men, usually from noble families, were taught to write on papyrus and carve symbols into stone. These men were called scribes. Scribes recorded great battles, business transactions, temple records and prayers, stories, and songs. Some scribes wrote letters for people who could not read or write.

The Calendar

The Nile helped Egyptians develop a calendar. Farming calendars plotted the rise and fall of the Nile's water, dividing the seasons according to its ebb and flow. In many ways, their division of the calendar year into three seasons is very similar to our own. As early as 3000 B.C., Egyptians had worked out a calendar of 365 days. It was based on the sun and had 12 thirty-day months plus five additional days. They invented this calendar by noting that the brightest star, Sirius, rose once a year, a moment or two before dawn. This seemed to predict the annual flood of the Nile and the ancient Egyptians fixed this event as the beginning of their calendar year.

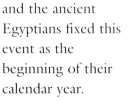

Written on stone

When Europeans explored Egypt in the 1700s, no one, including Egyptians of that time, could translate the writing and carvings. In 1798, while the French general Napoleon was fighting the British in Egypt, his soldiers discovered a black stone slab with three versions of the same message written on it. This slab was called the Rosetta Stone. It was the key that unlocked the mystery of a lost language. The stone was written in two forms of Egyptian followed by a Greek translation. Scholars who could read ancient Greek used it to understand the Egyptian hieroglyphs.

▲ *In 1822, a French scholar translated Egyptian hieroglyphs using inscriptions on the Rosetta Stone. The Rosetta Stone contains Greek, the everyday writing of ancient Egypt, called demotic, and hieroglyphs.*

◄ *This statue of a scribe was carved around 2400 B.C. When writing, scribes sat cross-legged and used their kilts, or skirts, as surfaces to write on. Scribes were very important people.*

Values and Beliefs

For thousands of years, the ancient Egyptians worshiped their pharaoh as a god. They worshiped other gods and goddesses, too. People believed that everything in life, from the arrival of spring each year to the loss of a lucky amulet **depended entirely on the attitudes of their gods.**

Gods and Goddesses

Amun-Re was the supreme god of ancient Egypt. He was also depicted as a sun god. The sun god was honored by all Egyptians because the sun made crops grow and brought life to the world. Other Egyptian gods were worshiped at specific times of the year or in different areas of the country. Some gods looked human, and some looked like animals. The god Harmakhis, or the Sphinx, looked like both. Fearsome traits of animals were associated with the gods' power over people. Thoth, god of learning and wisdom and the inventor of writing, had a human body but the head of an ibis, a bird with a long, slender bill. Hathor, goddess of love, childbirth, music, and dance, had a human form and a pair of cow's horns. Anubis, guardian of tombs, also had a human form but a jackal's head. Jackals were animals that prowled the graveyards, digging up human bones. Egyptians thought jackals knew how to guide and protect the dead on their journey to the **afterlife**.

The afterlife

The ancient Egyptians believed that after death, the spirit of a person traveled to heaven where it would live forever. The spirit was given many tests on its journey to the afterlife and the dead were buried with spells and charms to protect them. Before the journey could begin, the body had to be preserved through mummification. Mummies were buried with all of their precious possessions for the afterlife and food for the journey.

◀ *A coffin holds Pharaoh Tutenkhamen's organs.*

▲ *Horus, god of the sky, was often depicted as a falcon. He was said to have the moon as one eye and the sun as the other eye.*

18

Temples and Monuments

Pharaohs built massive temples from stone, where they believed gods and goddesses lived. Gods, like the dead, were thought to have the same needs as living people, including food, cleanliness, rest, and entertainment. Only the pharaoh and his priests and nobles were permitted inside the carved columns of temples to serve the gods or to attend ceremonies. Ordinary Egyptians never went closer than the outer courtyard.

▶ *The Temple of Karnak at Luxor was built over a period of several centuries. It was dedicated to the god Amun-Re, the chief god of Egypt and the protector of the pharaohs.*

▼ *The gigantic Sphinx, a lion with the face of a human, crouching in the desert near Giza, is depicted as Harmakhis, a form of the sun god.*

Life After Death

Ancient Egyptians believed the soul left the body at death but it later rejoined the body and stayed throughout eternity. Egyptians mummified their dead to preserve their bodies from decay and to give the soul a home.

1. It took about 70 days to mummify a body. First, embalmers removed the brain through the nose using a special curved hook.

2. Internal organs were removed next, but not the heart. It was believed that intelligence and emotions were contained in the heart, which was needed to pass a test posed by Osiris, god of the underworld, on the way to the afterlife, where they would live again.

3. After the organs were removed, the embalmers covered the body with natron salt, to dry it and prevent decay. The body then rested for 40 days. After 40 days, melted resin, or tree sap, was poured over the shriveled mummy to preserve the skin.

4. Organs that were needed for the afterlife were stored in jars.

5. The body was packed with sand, spices, and scented oil and linen, to give it shape. It took fifteen days to wrap the mummy.

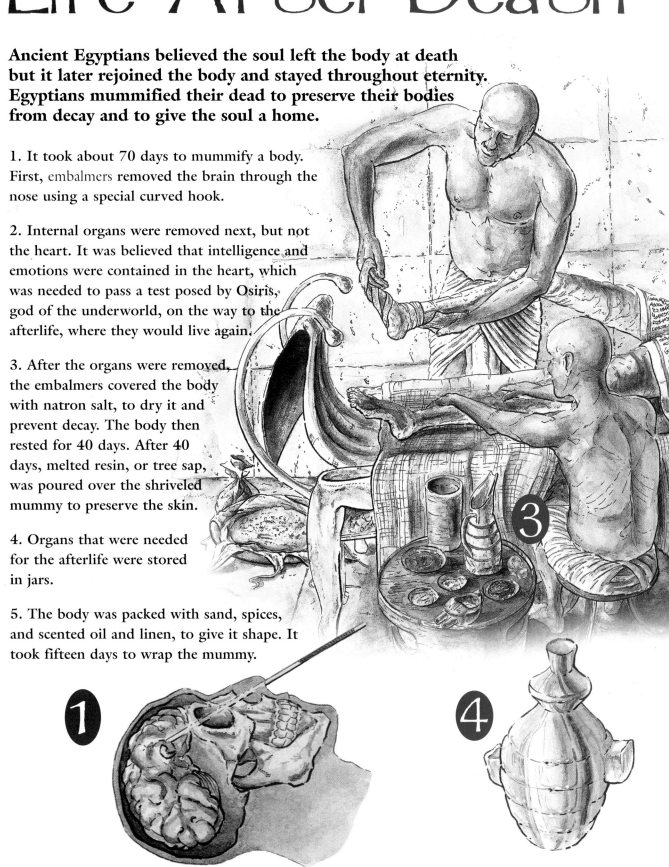

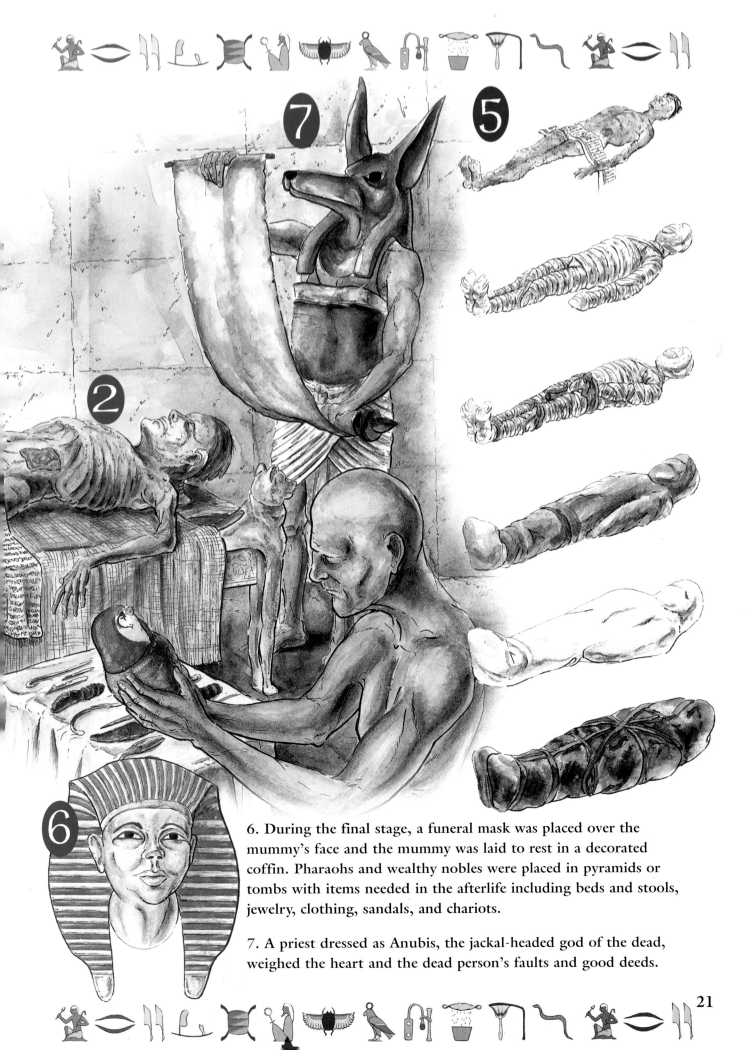

6. During the final stage, a funeral mask was placed over the mummy's face and the mummy was laid to rest in a decorated coffin. Pharaohs and wealthy nobles were placed in pyramids or tombs with items needed in the afterlife including beds and stools, jewelry, clothing, sandals, and chariots.

7. A priest dressed as Anubis, the jackal-headed god of the dead, weighed the heart and the dead person's faults and good deeds.

21

Arts and Pastimes

Ancient Egyptians held many celebrations throughout the year. They marked major events with feasts where musicians and dancers entertained. Egyptian artists painted scenes from these events on walls or tomb chapels.

Party!

Harvest and religious festivals were major events for the ancient Egyptians. The pharaoh and noble families held celebrations where guests dined on fattened cattle, wild fowl, wild antelope, gazelle, and ibex hunted nearby. Cooks prepared fancy meals using vegetables such as beans, lentils, herbs, and spices, along with a variety of fruits and coarse yeast bread. Guests drank ale made from barley, and wine made from grapes, dates, figs, and pomegranates.

Guests were welcomed to the parties with garlands of fresh flowers and perfumed water for washing their hands. Musicians and acrobats entertained people as they ate. Women put aromatic cones of fat on their headdresses and as it slowly melted, it bathed their wigs with sweet-smelling fragrance.

▲ *A woman plays a flute to entertain guests at a party. Other common Egyptian instruments included lyres, cymbals, drums, and harps.*

Games They Played

Egyptian children played with clay and wooden balls, tops, toy animals, and dolls. The games were made by craftspeople who handed their skills down to their children. Young and old enjoyed board games, especially a game called senet in which two players moved pieces around 30 squares on a wooden board. The winner was the first person to reach the kingdom of Osiris, god of the underworld.

For wealthy families, fishing was a favorite sport. They went on fishing expeditions in boats on the Nile. Wealthy Egyptians also hunted ducks, geese, and cranes in the papyrus reeds along the river. Hunting big game such as hippopotamus or crocodile required longer trips into the wilderness. Nobles also rode into the desert with packs of trained hunting dogs in pursuit of gazelle, antelope, foxes, and lions.

▲ *This board game was found in the tomb of an ancient Egyptian pharaoh. It is similar to a popular game called senet.*

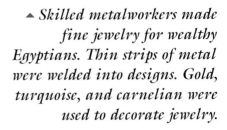

Design and Crafts

Objects of daily life, including sandals, rings, clothing, and drinking pots were made by leatherworkers, jewelers, cabinetmakers, weavers, and potters. Some of their work survives today. Gold and gems such as turquoise, carnelian, and amethyst were plentiful in ancient Egypt. Jewelers used them to decorate necklaces, bracelets and anklets. Wooden beds, carrying chairs, chariots and cosmetics boxes inlaid with **ivory** have been found in Egyptian tombs. The tomb of Pharaoh Tutenkhamen contained an **alabaster** vase to hold costly oils, royal daggers inlaid with bronze, and feathered fans.

▲ *Skilled metalworkers made fine jewelry for wealthy Egyptians. Thin strips of metal were welded into designs. Gold, turquoise, and carnelian were used to decorate jewelry.*

Religious Art

The Valley of the Kings is an area in central Egypt where many of the pharaohs of the New Kingdom (1600 B.C. to 1070 B.C.) were buried in tombs. Inside the tombs there were long corridors and secret rooms with walls covered in bright paintings. In the paintings, the pharaoh was depicted as a god. In some tombs, the artwork showed hunting scenes, farmers working the fields, dancing, games, animals, foreign visitors, and court ceremonies.

◀ *Throughout the country, Egyptians built statues of their god-king pharaoh. Sometimes the pharaoh was shown with his wife.*

Scientific Egypt

Ancient Egyptians tracked the annual floods of the Nile by recording them on paper. They also used simple math to create plans for irrigation projects that turned barren desert into farmland to feed a huge population.

Egyptian architects honored their pharaohs by building stone temples and pyramids. They found ways to accurately measure weights and distances, survey land, tell time, and calculate taxes to pay for the massive tributes to the pharaohs.

Farming Innovations

Egyptians measured their fields and estimated yields of grain to provide food for their enormous labor force and taxes for their pharaoh. The Egyptians also had vineyards where workers harvested and stomped on grapes to make wine for nobles who owned the estates. Ordinary people drank a nutritious beer made from wheat and barley.

Bringing Water to the Soil

The Nile river flooded every summer. If flood waters were too low for several years in a row, it would be too dry to farm and there would be famine. Flooding forced farmers and villagers from their homes near the banks to higher ground. Workers built dikes to keep the river from flooding villages.

Big catch basins were built to trap water as the floods receded. Workers dug canals leading from these basins so the water could be used in fields located farther away. By law, every citizen had to maintain the irrigation system. The wealthy paid others to do their share.

▲ *Egyptians gather papyrus reeds from the river's banks to make paper.*

Papermaking

Egyptians made an excellent lightweight paper from the stalk of the papyrus plant that grew on the banks of the Nile. Papyrus paper rolled up, and was far easier to handle than the heavy, baked clay tablets that other ancient cultures used to keep records. To make paper, workers cut ten-foot (three-meter) papyrus stems into shorter pieces and peeled them. After soaking in water, they were arranged in a double layer, covered with cloth and pounded with a mallet until the strips matted together. The sheets were polished with a rounded stone and then trimmed and pasted end-to-end into a roll ready for scribes to write on.

▲ *Irrigation methods developed by the ancient Egyptians are still used today.*

Nilometer

Egyptian engineers invented a device to check water levels on the Nile river. The nilometer was a gauge to measure the rise of the river. It was a wall of stone at the riverbank with markings, like a giant ruler standing on its end, accessible by steps. The water level was checked regularly, and at various locations. Knowing the rising or falling waters of the Nile was very important because all life depended on the Nile.

▼ *Egyptians used herbs to treat disease. Female druggists squeezed animal skins filled with herbs. Egyptians used this method to make herbal medicine.*

Sailing

Traffic was heavy on the Nile. Merchants, fishers, traders, stone haulers, and nobles all used the Nile to do their business. Egyptians constructed reed rafts for going through narrow canals and 200-foot (61-meter)long barges for hauling **obelisks**. They built boats to ferry people across the river. The wealthy relaxed on boats piloted by mariners on the Nile to catch the cooling breezes. Freighters carried grain up and down the river.

Medicine

Egyptians had knowledge of the body and how to heal wounds, mend broken bones, and treat diseases. One Egyptian doctor recorded a medical textbook on papyrus that described 48 cases of injury, including wounds and broken bones. The doctor wrote how he made a diagnosis by following some of the same methods that doctors use today, including watching the patient and applying ointments. Treatments included healing fractures with splints and casts. Egyptians had very little knowledge about internal medicine.

Inside a Pyramid

The Great Pyramid is the largest stone building ever built. It stands 482 feet (147 meters) high and is made from more than two million stone blocks.

Stone and Wood

In the desert west of the Nile, the engineers and builders of ancient Egypt developed a system for cutting stone to build pyramids, temples, and statues. In a huge rock face, workers carved holes and pounded wood wedges into them. They poured water over the wedges and the swelling of the wood caused the rock to crack and split. With chisels and mallets, stonecutters shaped the blocks of stone. Teams of men transported the blocks, which could weigh up to fifteen tons (fourteen tonnes), by sledge to barges waiting along the Nile.

Stone blocks of building material were unloaded from barges on the Nile to docks and construction storehouses near the pyramid building site.

Pyramids

The pyramid was the burial place of a pharaoh. Deep inside the gigantic monument, there was a special chamber where the pharaoh's body lay in its sarcofagus, or coffin. The pyramid contained secret passageways and rooms filled with burial goods and precious jewelry.

The great age of pyramid building lasted about 400 years. The first, built in 2630 B.C. for the powerful Pharaoh Djoser, was called the Step Pyramid because it looked like a massive staircase the king could use to climb to the sky after his death.

Less than 200 years later, the style had changed. The three pyramids at Giza looked like three-dimensional triangles with smooth sides. The largest now stands about 450 feet (137 meters) high. It required more than two million limestone blocks. The blocks weighed about two tons (1.8 tonnes) each, and were dragged by workers on oiled logs up earthen ramps. Up to 4,000 workers were used to drag the blocks up the ramps and set them in place.

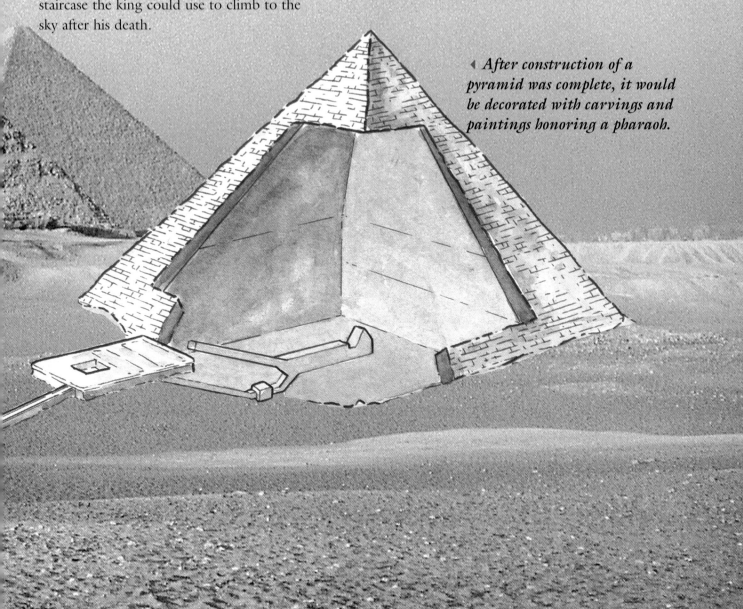

◄ *After construction of a pyramid was complete, it would be decorated with carvings and paintings honoring a pharaoh.*

The Fall of Egypt

Egyptians were one of the earliest ancient peoples to weave the threads of civilization into a lasting nation. Its temples and pyramids still stand and amaze people today, after more than 5,000 years. Ancient Egypt survived wars, droughts, and famines but finally fell to outside invaders.

The War Within

For a time, the desert surrounding the Nile delta and arable lands along the river banks discouraged attackers. After about 1190 B.C., the pharaoh found himself defending his land instead of invading other nations. Egypt was repeatedly attacked by a people from the Mediterranean, who the Egyptians called the "Sea People." The attacks weakened Egypt and around 1050 B.C., the country divided. For the next 300 years, several cultures claimed leadership but no one was in control of the whole region of ancient Egypt.

For many years, Egypt had been paying foreigners to defend its borders. Many were Libyans who were given land as payment for their services. In 950 B.C., a Libyan named Sheshonk conquered Upper and Lower Egypt. His family ruled for about 200 years.

Nubian Rule

In about 730 B.C., the Nubians, who ruled a kingdom to the south, invaded Egypt. The Nubians ruled Egypt for almost 100 years.

▸ *Invaders known as the "Sea People" attacked Egypt from across the Mediterranean Sea.*

Invasion

Egypt's next invader came from Assyria, to the east, where the modern country of Iraq is located. The Assyrians were the fiercest warriors of the time. They made weapons out of iron, a much stronger metal than the copper Egyptians used for their spears, shields, knives, and daggers.

After capturing Egypt, the Assyrians withdrew to fight elsewhere. They left an Egyptian prince named Psammetichus to rule Egypt for them. Psammetichus invited other foreigners to settle in Egypt. In 525 B.C., invaders from Persia, or modern Iran, captured Egypt. Alexander the Great entered Egypt with his army in 332 B.C. After he forced the Persians from Egypt, the Egyptians treated him as a hero.

Alexander moved Egypt's capital to a new city by the Mediterranean Sea named Alexandria. After his death, a dynasty of kings, who were all named Ptolemy, ruled from Alexandria. They made Greek the official language of Egypt. Greek soldiers, government workers, and businessmen arrived in Egypt and took the most important jobs. During Greek rule, the Egyptian religion was honored and temples continued to be built for their gods.

▲ *Alexander the Great was a great warrior who ruled a vast empire.*

▼ *An Assyrian carving, called a bas-relief, shows invaders under King Ashurbanipal scaling a fort wall in Egypt in about 640 B.C.*

The Final Blow

By 200 B.C., the Roman Empire had begun to conquer the ancient peoples of the Mediterranean. By 50 B.C., Rome was strong enough to force Egypt to do as it asked without invading Egypt. Julius Caesar, the Emperor of Rome, made Egypt's young queen Cleopatra his mistress. When Caesar died, two Roman leaders, Octavian and Marc Antony competed to take control of Rome. Cleopatra became Marc Antony's mistress. When Cleopatra and Marc Antony were defeated in battle by Octavian's army, they committed suicide. Cleopatra was ancient Egypt's last ruler. With her death, one of the greatest civilizations of the ancient world had come to an end. Octavian celebrated his conquest by changing his name to Augustus and Egypt became part of the Roman Empire.

▶ *Queen Cleopatra was the last ruler of ancient Egypt. She was one of ancient Egypt's most famous rulers but she was not Egyptian. She was a descendant of Ptolemy, a Greek general who conquered Egypt.*

▼ *In 30 B.C., the Roman Emperor Octavian defeated the combined forces of Roman General Marc Antony and Cleopatra, the last queen of Egypt, at the Battle of Actium.*

Protecting Egyptian Heritage

An Egyptian saying states that "everyone fears the passage of time, but time fears the pyramids." The pyramids have survived the harsh climate of Egypt, war, and pollution. Today, Egyptian authorities are working hard to preserve these monuments but they cannot do much about the artifacts they used to contain. European explorers began to dig up Egyptian artifacts in the 1800s. Since then, European archaeologists called Egyptologists, who specialized in Egypt, found and sent back home important Egyptian artifacts. Museums around the world have valuable collections of Egyptian art, mummies, and burial objects taken by early Egyptologists, or by tourists. Today, Egypt does not allow archaeologists to take objects out of the country. Sometimes, grave robbers and smugglers steal the artifacts and offer them for sale outside the country. Egypt has asked that these items be returned. It has also set up a special committee to look into stolen antiquities, or ancient treasures. Several important artifacts have been returned, including the mummy of Ramses I, which was looted from the Valley of the Kings in 1871. It is against the law to buy an Egyptian artifact in Egypt today. Visitors and tourists cannot take artifacts home anymore.

▲ *British soldiers and their Egyptian guides and porters pose on the Sphinx in the 1800s. The Great Sphinx had a body of a male lion and the head of a human.*

Glossary

afterlife A life believed in many religions to continue after death

alabaster A type of hard white stone

amulet An object or piece of jewelry worn around the neck as a charm against injury or evil

bartered To trade goods without exchanging money

conquer To take over by force

court A pharaoh or king and all those around him, including his family, personal servants, advisors, and officials

cultures Beliefs, traditions, and behaviors that are unique to a group of people

embalmers People who prevent the decay of dead bodies by treating them with preservatives before burying them

fertile Good soil for plants to grow in

generation a group of people born or living at the same time

inherit To receive property and possessions after one's death

irrigate to supply land with water for crops through ditches, human-made channels, or sprinklers

ivory A white bone-like substance from the tusks of animals such as elephants

minerals Naturally occurring, non-living substances such as as diamonds or crystals

nobles Members of the wealthiest, or most powerful group in society, called the nobility

nomadic hunters People who move from place to place, following herds of wild animals that they hunt and depend on for food

obelisks Columns, or shafts with four sides that usually come to a point at the top and are sometimes engraved or carved

priests People who lead or perform religious ceremonies

pastures Land used for animal grazing

pyramids Huge structure that usually have a square base and four triangular sides meeting at a point

Roman Empire A group of territories under the control and rule of Rome. Rome conquered Egypt in 30 B.C.

Index

1 2 3 4 5 6 7 8 9 0 Printed in the U.S.A. 0 9 8 7 6 5 4